Jeffrey Dahmer

The Gruesome True Story of a
Hungry Cannibalistic Rapist and Necrophiliac
Serial Killer

Real Crime by Real Killers Volume 3

Second Edition

Ryan Becker, True Crime Seven

TRUE CRIME 7

ISBN: 9781978493254

Table of Contents

Explore the Stories of

The Murderous Minds

A Note

From True Crime Seven

Hi there!

Thank you so much for picking up our book! Before you continue your exploration into the dark world of killers, we wanted to take a quick moment to explain the purpose of our books.

Our goal is to simply explore and tell the stories of various killers in the world: from unknown murderers to infamous serial killers. Our books are designed to be short and inclusive; we want to tell a good scary true story that anyone can enjoy regardless of their reading level.

That is why you won't see too many fancy words or complicated sentence structures in our books. Also, to prevent the typical cut and dry style of true crime books, we try to keep the narrative easy to follow while incorporating fiction style storytelling. As to information, we often find ourselves with too little or too much. So, in terms of research material and content, we always try to include what further helps the story of the killer.

Lastly, we want to acknowledge that, much like history, true crime is a subject that can often be interpreted differently. Depending on the topic and your upbringing, you might agree or disagree with how we present a story. We understand disagreements are inevitable. That is why we added this note so hopefully, it can help you better understand our position and goal.

Now without further ado, let the exploration to the dark begin!

Introduction

A PLANET WITH A POPULATION OF OVER SEVEN billion is bound to produce moments of greatness. These are events, which, for better or for worse, mark the course of humanity and change it forever.

Throughout the existence of humankind, we have witnessed and recorded these moments: destructive wars, terrible disasters, heroic last stands, heartwarming acts, the creation of impressive structures, and amazing adventures.

Earth has seen it all, and it has learned from these moments in time.

All these moments have something in common. Individuals, equally great men and women, whose names remain in our history and our memories forever, brought these moments to life.

There are people whose names we remember for the good they brought to the world; they made our planet a better place while here, and we sorely miss them when they are gone. Some well-known people are more controversial than others—some are hated—while others are loved. These include conquerors, kings, queens, and perhaps even rock stars; one way or another, these famous people had an impact on our history.

The following book will not discuss such characters.

No. The subject of this book is not just a man shrouded in greatness—great evil that is—but also one who did not leave goodness behind him after his death. He left no positive legacy, nor lessons for the people who knew him to learn. His name strikes terror and disgust in those who hear it, and anybody who was ever around him still trembles in fear at the mention of his name.

Every so often, humanity spawns monsters—beasts disguised by human skin—who care little for their fellow beings and wish only to satisfy their own needs. These are killers, rapists, torturers, and other criminals who are spawned from the dark, to bring pain and distress to those around them.

Even then, some are more ruthless and despicable than others in this group. There are big names—celebrities of murder, so to speak—even among those who cause pain.

This book is about one of the biggest of these names—a monster that is known worldwide and feared universally.

The subject of the following book is a man who brought pain and suffering to a large number of victims. He never felt a shred of pity or remorse for what he had done or the way his actions ruined the lives of the many families and friends of those he killed.

This killer took seventeen lives: seventeen victims who did not go quietly.

The man who killed these poor souls saw them simply as 'things.' They were objects to pleasure him as he raped and brutalized them, watching intently as their lives seeped out of their bodies.

His name, of course, is **Jeffrey Dahmer**. This monster, known as the Milwaukee Cannibal, was a killer who began to hurt living beings as early as childhood. Dahmer enjoyed every second of his murders—from the abductions, the preservation, and even the consumption of his victims.

Yet, the biggest issue with Dahmer was not necessarily what he did, but the fact that he was *good at it*, and could not bring himself to stop.

Now is the moment for you to discover the tale of one of America's worst killers. If you are faint of heart, consider putting this book down to prepare yourself before starting to read; the grisly details will not be spared.

There is no shortage of material on Jeffrey Dahmer from various sources: books, magazines, even on the internet. However, this is not merely recounting his life story and the murders. Rather, it is a push into the abyss of Dahmer's mind. You see, this book will change you, for better or for worse.

The horrific tale of Jeffrey Dahmer and his murders is about to begin.

I

The Loss of Innocence

BEFORE WE BEGIN, THE FOLLOWING MUST BE said, if only to separate our killer from other monsters — to take away the possibility of doubt or pity. Jeffrey Dahmer, unlike many others who have become serial killers, was not born into an abusive household, nor forced into what he became by terrible poverty and bad influences.

Jeffrey could have become whatever he wished, but he chose to become a killer. And not just any killer: *One of the worst killers the world has ever seen.*

Our story begins on the 21st of May in 1960. Jeffrey Lionel Dahmer was born in West Allis, Wisconsin, to Joyce Annette and

Lionel Herbert Dahmer. Joyce was a teletype machine instructor, while Lionel studied analytical chemistry at Marquette University.

As a baby, Jeffrey received all the attention a child could wish for; his parents took good care of him. However, as the years passed and their marriage became tense, Lionel and Joyce began to somewhat neglect him. The disruption in the marriage was due in part to Joyce's personality. Being the type of person who continuously demanded attention, Joyce would go as far as faking sickness to get responsiveness.

It did not help that Lionel was very busy with his studies, spending extended periods of time away from home, only to return to his wife, feigning a nervous breakdown.

Despite initially being a happy and playful child, a change occurred after Jeffery underwent double hernia surgery at the age of six. He became quieter and more subdued.

In school, Jeffrey was considered to be a quiet and shy boy; he showed signs of neglect but had fortunately managed to make some friends. While there are claims that a neighbor molested Jeffrey at some point in his younger years, no one has confirmed these allegations. Dahmer himself later recalled having been present on several occasions when his parents argued. These scenes were upsetting for a child. Fortunately, Dahmer's parents' love for him did not change at any point.

As a young boy, Jeffrey fell completely in love with animals. The family had a pet dog, and, at one point, they helped nurse a bird back to health from an injury. Lionel would later recall Jeffrey watched the bird fly away into the wild with "wide, gleaming eyes," and it had probably been the happiest moment in his life.

Shortly after, Jeffrey came upon his father, sweeping some animal bones out from under their home. He felt intensely curious when he saw the body parts and asked his father what they were. Lionel noticed when Jeffrey heard the crunching noises the bones made, he seemed oddly thrilled, requesting to touch them himself. Later, Lionel would come to understand this was the very first sign of what his son would eventually become.

In 1966, Lionel graduated then found a job as a research chemist. Unfortunately for the family, this would require them to uproot and move to Akron, Ohio. Joyce was pregnant with their second son, David. Her pregnancy was a troublesome one, making her weak and prone to sickness. Jeffrey, now seven, gradually received less and less attention, and he began to lose self-confidence and his previously bubbly nature diminished.

Soon, even the very idea of starting a new school made Jeffrey fearful. Lionel tried not to worry, hoping Jeffrey had just not adapted to his new home yet. In reality, it was far more than that.

After buying and moving into a new home in April 1967, young Jeffrey seemed to begin to get used to his new life, even finding a new friend named Lee. Jeffrey also grew close to a female teacher, who he eventually gifted a bowl of tadpoles he had caught on his own. Later, however, he would find out his teacher had given the bowl to Lee. This event angered Jeffrey and led him to sneak into the boy's garage to poison the animals' water with motor oil, killing all of them.

This occasion was not the last time Jeffrey came into contact with dead animals.

The young Dahmer was fascinated with hunting his neighborhood for the corpses of critters. He often took them home and dissected them, sometimes getting rid of the bones in the woods near his home to avoid raising suspicion. When he went fishing with his father, Jeffrey's favorite part of the activity was cutting open the fish and gutting them. Nobody paid attention to this proclivity.

One night, during a family dinner of chicken, Jeffrey asked his father what would happen if he put the chicken bones in a bleach

18

solution. His father, pleasantly surprised by his child's curiosity, decided to teach him how to bleach animal bones, safely and correctly. There was no harm in it, his father thought. After all, it was merely a childish curiosity. His father was most likely relieved by Jeffrey's request since he had shown such little interest in other hobbies up to this point.

Had someone known what was really happening, Dahmer's story may have ended very differently.

Jeffrey wasn't just inspecting the insides of animal corpses and preserving their bones for science.

He was getting ready for something much worse.

II

An Odd Young Man

JEFFREY'S HIGH SCHOOL YEARS ARRIVED, AND HE began to grow in stature. As a tall, awkward youth, he shifted from random quiet, shy states to extroverted ones. He developed a penchant for playing crude practical jokes when he was drunk; this habit would continue throughout the years up to Jeffrey's death.

Classmates stated that Dahmer would arrive to class looking disheveled, with a can or two of beer in his bag, to consume during class. A curious classmate once asked him why he was continuously drinking during class, to which Dahmer responded: "It's my medicine."

His jokes were cruel. He often mimicked his mother's interior designer, who had cerebral palsy, to the enjoyment of many of his peers. Other times he would paint chalk outlines in the halls of his school, reminiscent of those found at crime scenes once law enforcement removed the body.

Jeffrey was considered to be intelligent and polite but regularly received average grades due to his extreme apathy and lack of interest in studying or reading. His parents hired a private tutor, but nothing changed. Dahmer was not willing to make an effort, so there was little the tutor could do.

It was around this age that Dahmer discovered two important things that would define him as a human being and mold him into what he would become later.

The first was that he was gay. Jeffrey first noticed it as a small attraction towards other men, but even in these early stages of realization, Dahmer kept it from his parents. He had a brief relationship with another boy, but it did not get very far.

Then he had a second, separate realization. Dahmer began to fantasize about dominating another male, taking complete control, doing whatever he wanted to a partner, without their consent.

Jeffrey wanted to hurt somebody, to make sexual use of them, and perhaps kill and dissect them in the process. The limits of sex and dissection began to blur, as Dahmer included one within the other in his fantasies. His desire for violence became so overwhelming, and he began to make plans for his first victim.

The idea that would finally spark Jeffrey's killer instinct came to fruition. On several occasions, Dahmer had spotted a male jogger he found attractive. He knew the man's route passed by a section of thick bushes. Dahmer had the perfect place to hide, as well as the perfect opportunity to take advantage of his victim if he could successfully render him unconscious.

After fantasizing about this idea, Dahmer decided to make his fantasy come true. Armed with a baseball bat, he went to the bushes and lay in wait, patiently expecting the jogger. To the man's extreme good fortune, he did not jog that route on that particular day, and Dahmer decided to give up on his fantasy. If the would-be victim had passed through the bushy area, Dahmer almost certainly would have followed through with his plan.

In the Dahmer household, Lionel and Joyce's marriage was deteriorating. The couple had less and less patience for each other. Arguments were becoming a regular event, and Jeffrey was having a hard time seeing them fight. His drinking increased; he became more despondent as time passed.

Jeffrey's terrible and secret habit of dissecting and skinning animals became the only thing that motivated him. His parents and other grown-ups watched as his peers spoke of dreams, careers, and plans, while Dahmer sunk further into apathy and purposelessness. Jeffrey was more comfortable lying on his bed alone in his room than making an effort in his studies or looking for a job. At this point, even interacting with other people had become a challenge for him.

Even worse, nobody could detect what Jeffrey was truly harboring on the inside because of his guarded and closed nature. He did not argue with anyone, never got involved in his parents' increasingly common fights, and kept his strange habits secret enough for everyone to find him merely different—not actually troubled or sick

When Jeffrey was almost eighteen, his parents finally gave up on their marriage and got divorced. Where Joyce had been a self-centered woman with barely any attention for Jeffrey, Lionel's new fiancée, Shari, was more attentive toward the boy. She recommended that Jeffrey start college after high school, and Lionel agreed.

It looked like Jeffrey was going to turn over a new leaf. He seemed as though he might get an education that could help him progress as a human being. Jeffrey had a chance to start over and become a regular person, despite his awkward teenage years and childhood.

Unfortunately, Jeffrey's fate was about to darken. He was about to let loose the demon who inhabited his mind. Jeffrey Dahmer was about to become the killer the world would remember; the construction of a horrific legacy was about to begin.

III

A Taste of Blood

JEFFREY GRADUATED FROM HIGH SCHOOL IN THE summer of 1978. He was now eighteen years old. Lionel Dahmer had gone on a business trip with his new wife, while Jeffrey's mother, Joyce, and younger brother, David, had relocated to Wisconsin.

Jeffrey was left alone at home with his dark thoughts and darker desires. It was just a matter of time before he acted on them.

It wouldn't take long.

Just three weeks after graduating, with nobody around to supervise him or give him a moment of pause before making a rash decision—that he would never be able to take back, Jeffrey Dahmer took his first life.

Eighteen-year-old Steven Mark Hicks would become Dahmer's first victim. Dahmer had imagined picking up a male hitchhiker and killing him. Not only did he have the freedom to do so, but as it happened, Hicks was hitchhiking as Dahmer was out looking for someone to fulfill his fantasy.

After exchanging a few words, Jeffrey invited Hicks to his home for some beers. Steven agreed, unaware that Dahmer wanted to unleash his macabre desires on him.

When the two arrived at Dahmer's home, he pulled out some alcohol from the fridge, put some rock music on the radio, and began enjoying Hicks' company.

However, at some point in the conversation, Dahmer realized that Steven was not gay like himself. There was an awkward exchange, at which Steven said he wanted to go home. Dahmer thought he had heard wrong. *Go home?* Why would his victim want to go home? This request was awkward for Dahmer; he had so many things in mind for the night. Hicks was about to ruin it all by leaving.

Something snapped in Dahmer's mind. He approached Steven from behind while he was sitting down. Dahmer held a ten-pound dumbbell in his hand. Hicks had no time to react as Dahmer slammed the heavy object into his head twice, knocking him unconscious.

However, the bludgeoning was not the end of the attack. Dahmer knelt over Steven's body, strangling him to death with the bar of his rudimentary weapon. Then he stripped the fresh corpse of its clothes and masturbated over it with sick pleasure.

Jeffrey Dahmer had finally acted on his fantasies, and the sensation felt strange. While part of him wanted to weep over what he had done, another part was glad that he had finally followed through on years of dark fantasies. It was a mix of emotions. Dahmer was not in a hurry to kill again... yet.

The next day, Dahmer was finally able to put into practice what he had been learning for years. Dragging the body downstairs to a crawl space, he dissected it and buried the remains in a shallow grave in his backyard. Several weeks later, he would exhume the body parts, remove the flesh from the bones, dissolve it in acid, and flush the remaining solution down the toilet.

Six weeks later, Lionel and Shari returned home. They found Jeffrey home alone—doing nothing productive with his life. He agreed to enroll at Ohio State University, majoring in business.

Initially, his father had high hopes for his son. However, Dahmer wasted no time proving he was not going to stop abusing alcohol anytime soon. With no accomplishments at the University, he quit before even completing his first term. Dahmer was back slouching around at home.

Lionel would not tolerate Jeffrey's apathy. If he was not going to study, there was space in the Army for him. In January 1979, Jeffrey Dahmer enlisted in the U.S. Army. He trained to become a medical specialist at Fort Sam, Houston. Considered an effective soldier, he was stationed in Baumholder, West Germany, a few months later.

Once there, Dahmer fulfilled the role of a combat medic. It was not the ideal position for him since he could not stand looking at blood, a strange detail that psychologists would later explain as guilt over Steven Hick's murder, but Dahmer tried his best to perform the required duties.

While the Army officially recorded his performance as a soldier as being "average or above average," there were some ugly rumors about Dahmer, that in retrospect, chill the blood.

In 2010, one soldier said that Dahmer had repeatedly raped him during a seventeen-month period, while another stated he had been drugged and raped by Dahmer in an armored vehicle in 1979.

Alcoholism and loneliness continued to drag Dahmer down, and he was eventually declared unfit for service. The Army formally and honorably discharged him in March 1981. Not long after, Dahmer was sent to Fort Jackson for debriefing. As part of his release from service, the military subsequently provided Dahmer with a ticket to a destination of his choice, anywhere in the country.

Deciding where to go was tough for Dahmer. Ultimately, he felt he had disappointed his father too much to return to Ohio. He did not want to return there with his tail between his legs. Determined to live by his own means, Dahmer chose to travel to Miami Beach, Florida, where he got a job at a sandwich place. Nobody would have guessed that the tall young man preparing their lunch was a killer, who would soon go on to become legendary among murderers.

Dahmer's alcoholism was ever-present, despite having a stable job. However, Jeffrey found himself unable to keep up with his responsibilities. His landlord evicted him for missing rent payments. Now the young man knew he only had one person to turn to, so he called his father, asking if he could return to live with him in Ohio. Lionel accepted.

Coming home was a source of simultaneous comfort and discomfort for Dahmer. While his return allowed him to walk around familiar territory, it also reminded him of what he had done to Steven Hicks; one detail nagged at him, causing him to worry about getting caught.

As soon as he had the chance to be home alone, Dahmer unearthed the bones he had buried in his father's backyard and took a sledgehammer to them, pulverizing the body parts completely and scattering them in the woodlands behind the family home.

As Dahmer disposed of the bones, he hoped that his murder experimentation had ended—that he would recover from his dark fantasies. Unfortunately for both him and future victims, he had only temporarily quashed these dreams of control, pain, and murder.

In fact, they would all come flooding back at any moment…

IV

No Escaping Who You Are

ONLY THREE WEEKS AFTER HAVING RETURNED to Ohio, in October 1981, Jeffrey messed up again, frustrating his father and stepmother tenfold.

After drinking too much, Jeffrey was arrested for drunken and disorderly conduct. Lionel was not as forgiving as on previous occasions. He and his wife decided Jeffrey had to go elsewhere to truly start over.

While he had mostly been a cold, quiet boy during his life, Jeffrey had shown to carry an affection for his grandmother, Lionel's mother. Lionel hoped that Jeffrey could start over at her home in

West Allis, Wisconsin—thinking a change of scenery could help Jeffrey become more responsible and mature.

Moving to West Allis, Jeffrey Dahmer immediately adapted to a new, calmer life than the one experienced in both Ohio and Florida. His grandmother paid more attention to his behavior than his parents ever had. He accompanied her to many activities and helped her out with a variety of chores. His only trouble obeying his grandmother was with quitting alcohol, but professionally, his life took a general turn for the better. He even found a decent job at a blood plasma center, where he helped collect blood from donors.

Meanwhile, Dahmer's personal life continued to decline. His behavior became increasingly stranger, worrying his grandmother. At one point, she entered Jeffrey's room and was shocked to find a fully-dressed male mannequin in his closet. He had been using it as a sex toy of some kind. She also discovered a .357 Magnum under his bed. The elderly woman was not sure if he was capable of using the firearm because Dahmer had never shown her his violent side. Eventually, she would ask Dahmer to throw it away.

In 1982, Dahmer was arrested for indecent exposure in front of a crowd of over twenty-five women and children. He was convicted and fined fifty dollars, plus court costs. Lionel was always there to pay whatever costs were generated by Dahmer's mistakes. Time and again, he crossed his fingers, hoping his son would change his ways. Interestingly, this undying hope became a recurring pattern that Lionel repeated even after Jeffrey was caught. He had a warm heart when it came to his son, despite the constant disappointments.

In January 1985, Dahmer gained employment as a mixer at the Milwaukee Ambrosia Chocolate Factory, where he worked eight hours, at nine dollars an hour, six nights a week. He enjoyed the job and the freedom that came with it. Around this time, he visited the West Allis Public Library, spending some of his time off reading books and newspaper articles.

His dark fantasies were reignited there.

While at the library one day, a man walked past Dahmer and lay a note on his table, offering to perform fellatio on Dahmer. Despite Dahmer not answering the man's note, it aroused him. He recalled the fantasies of being in control and dominant.

Consequently, Dahmer started to actively seek out sexual partners at gay bars, bookstores, and bathhouses in the area, trying to find men interested in fulfilling his desires. Ultimately, he preferred the bathhouses for their added privacy, increased intimacy, and a relaxing atmosphere.

First, Dahmer used the bathhouses to find consensual sexual partners but soon began to feel uncomfortable and frustrated when his lovers moved and made noises while he was pleasuring them. As previously stated, Dahmer required total control and dominance; acts of sexual intercourse were no different. From Dahmer's perspective, other men were simply objects of pleasure, not people. As a result, he thought of ways to reduce the influence that a partner had during sex and began to purchase sleeping pills.

Dahmer engaged in consensual acts of intercourse until June 1986, where his curiosity overwhelmed him, and he began to drug his victims by lacing their beverages with sedatives. Then he took advantage of their bodies, raping them with no regard for their comfort or consent. This pattern occurred a dozen times until the bathhouse's administration grew wary of him and revoked his membership. Additionally, they barred Dahmer from ever entering the bathhouse again. However, no one pressed charges, so Jeffrey Dahmer simply walked away from his violent crimes without consequence.

Around this time, Dahmer read in the newspaper about the funeral of an eighteen-year-old male, who had recently died and been buried. He saw the boy's picture and imagined himself raping the corpse, which aroused him. He visited the grave one night with a spade and began to dig, but found the soil too hard to penetrate and decided to abort his plan.

That same year, police arrested Dahmer again for indecent exposure. He was caught masturbating in front of two boys, near the Kinnickinnic River, in August. The police brought him into the station for questioning. Although he initially admitted he had been pleasuring himself, he later changed the story to state that he was only urinating when witnesses spotted him. The prosecution changed the charges to disorderly conduct and the court sentenced Dahmer to a one-year probation, as well as a series of counseling visits.

Law enforcement had already arrested Dahmer twice, and yet again, nobody recognized his sinister capacity. This oversight continued to occur on further occasions, with family members, neighbors, and even law enforcement officers failing to see beyond his quiet, shy façade, to spot the monster lurking behind. The real Dahmer, for all his fantasies and one murder victim already to his name, was invisible to everyone around him.

Jeffrey's murderous tendencies had been dormant for years, but a mixture of factors had reawakened his true nature and brought out his urges again. His ability to blend in, coupled with Dahmer's blatant disregard for getting caught, acted as a useful tactic for him.

It was one that would soon come in handy when, once again, he began to kill.

V

Reawakened

NINE YEARS.

It had been over nine years since 1978 when Dahmer had killed hitchhiker Steven Hicks. In the interim, Dahmer had drugged and raped men, been arrested twice for indecent exposure, yet he had not killed again.

Unfortunately, this grace period was approaching its end.

Dahmer regularly brought partners home to his grandmother's house in West Allis, to have sex. However, on one occasion in November 1987, after having his bathhouse permit revoked, Dahmer visited a gay bar in search of someone to take to a hotel.

There, he met twenty-five-year-old Steven Tuomi from Michigan, and sadly he would become Dahmer's second murder victim.

Dahmer stated that he had only intended to drug Steven, rape him while he was unconscious, and then part ways with him the next morning, never to see him again.

However, events did not go as planned.

According to Dahmer, he awoke the next morning to find Tuomi lying under him; the man's chest had caved in and was heavily bruised. Dahmer's own forearm was also very bruised, his fists bloody. Dahmer states he sat there in shock, looking at the corpse, and his own hands, trying to find an explanation. He claimed he did not remember killing Tuomi and stuck with this story to his grave, never confessing to committing the murder.

In fact, Dahmer always argued he did not remember anything about the night of Tuomi's death. He explained when he woke to find Tuomi dead, only one thing mattered to him—getting rid of the corpse. Dahmer had registered the hotel room in his own name and realized detection would mean getting locked up for real.

Dahmer left the hotel briefly to purchase a large suitcase, which he used to store Tuomi's body in, before calling a cab. Successfully avoiding detection in the hotel's lobby, Dahmer checked out and walked to the taxi waiting for him. The driver helped him get the suitcase into the vehicle.

To which the taxi driver complained about the weight, asking, "What's in here, a corpse?"

Jeffrey Dahmer smiled knowingly and nodded, and the driver finished putting the suitcase in the car before setting off to Dahmer's grandmother's home.

The corpse remained in his grandmother's basement for an entire week, during which time Dahmer had sex with it, masturbated on it, and finally began to dismember it to dispose of the evidence. He began by severing the head, arms, and legs from the torso, before filleting the bones from the body and dicing the flesh into small pieces. He moved the flesh to garbage bags, while the bones were placed in a sheet and ground into splinters with the same sledgehammer he had used for his first victim's body. Two hours later, Dahmer had destroyed Steven Tuomi's remains completely, except for the victim's head.

For a while, Dahmer kept Tuomi's head as a trophy, storing it in a blanket. Then he boiled and treated it with a mix of industrial detergent and bleach to preserve the skull. His obsession with bones had never truly gone away, and now he used the skull as stimulation for arousal and masturbation. It eventually grew too brittle to manipulate, and Dahmer was forced to take his sledgehammer to it and throw the remains away. Law enforcement officials never found them.

While he had previously felt guilty for killing Steven Hicks, Dahmer did not feel the same about Tuomi. Confused? Perhaps. Certainly, not guilty, however. He had even had some fun disposing of the body. His beloved grandmother was none the wiser.

Tuomi's murder buoyed Dahmer's previously-dwindling desire to kill. Now, he began actively searching for victims. Visiting gay bars, he used his established method: offer his victims money to pose for photographs, or simply have a drink and watch some movies with him at home—before actually taking them to his grandmother's, strangling them after drugging and raping them. Just like while they were living, he considered male corpses sexual objects. He often penetrated and masturbated on them. Dahmer also kept trophies from the victims' bodies, thinking of the skull as the most important body part a victim could leave him.

Steven Tuomi was the last murder victim that Dahmer disposed of quickly and without much fuss. The reality is, Jeffrey

Dahmer was not an 'average' or a simple killer. Whereas the actual process of hunting a victim and taking their life is the thrill for most murderers, to Dahmer, this was only the prelude to the joyous experience which came after.

Similar to other serial killers, with control and domination forces pushing Dahmer to continue killing, He differed significantly in that he was not interested in hearing a victim beg, or watching them despair as he cut or killed them. He ended lives quickly, was very subtle in his intentions, and even helped them to go more 'easily' by drugging them.

In truth, Dahmer was more of a necrophiliac than anything else; he just took things a step further by creating the corpses for himself.

Two months after murdering Steven Tuomi, Dahmer met James Doxtator, a fourteen-year-old, who was working as a male sex worker. Dahmer lured the boy to his home with an offer of fifty dollars, to take some nude photographs.

James was only a child, Dahmer would soon add him to his growing pile of the dead.

The killing spree was about to begin.

VI

Killing Spree

DOXTATOR WAS YOUNG AND NAÏVE. HE WENT to Dahmer's West Allis residence without a second thought. There, he and Dahmer had sex, and the murderer then drugged the boy. While James was sedated, Dahmer strangled him on the floor of his grandmother's cellar.

Dahmer left the corpse alone for a week before dismembering it, having used the body as a source of sexual stimulation and masturbating on it regularly. He disposed of the body parts in the trash, separating the skull from the rest and keeping it. He boiled it in the same solution he had used with Tuomi. Dahmer kept the skull for a while before using his sledgehammer to pulverize it.

Dahmer's next victim was twenty-two-year-old Richard Guerrero, a bisexual man he met outside a gay bar on March 24, 1988.

Dahmer may have been a shy young man during his teenage years, but when he wanted to lure a victim to their death, he was quite outgoing. All it took was an offer of fifty dollars and a night of sex to get Richard to follow him home. They were soon on their way to Dahmer's grandmother's house. There, Dahmer used a leather strap to strangle the life out of a sedated Guerrero, who had a drink laced with sleeping pills. Just like that, Dahmer had taken the lives of four men. This time, he felt immediately aroused at seeing Guerrero's corpse and began to perform oral sex on the body.

Twenty-four hours later, Dahmer dismembered the man's corpse, separated the skull to keep as a trophy. It would remain in Dahmer's possession for several more months until he decided to pulverize it with his sledgehammer.

On April 23, 1988, just one month after killing Guerrero, Dahmer struck again. He lured a young man from a gay bar to his grandmother's home and invited him in for coffee. The beverage contained several sleeping pills, which Dahmer used to sedate the man, just as he had done with his previous victims. However, as

Dahmer waited for the drugs to take their effect, he heard his grandmother moving around in the room above them.

"Is that you, Jeff?" she called out. Dahmer awkwardly replied that he was alone, but correctly guessed that his grandmother did not believe him. He decided not to take any risks and was left frustrated as his victim lost consciousness. Dahmer did not hurt, rape, or murder the young man, instead choosing to take him to County General Hospital before returning home.

Dahmer continued to bring men to his grandmother's home, although without killing anyone else, for an extended period. Eventually, this arrangement became unacceptable to her. She had already expressed her discomfort with strangers being in her home, as well as the horrible smells that regularly came up from the cellar.

On one occasion, she even found a strange black sticky substance on the cellar floor, emitting a foul smell. Jeffrey's only answer was he had been experimenting on animals, and left it at that. But his grandmother had finally had enough, and at the beginning of September 1988, she asked her grandson to find a new place to live.

Dahmer did not take long to find a place.

His new home was a one-bedroom apartment, where he moved on September 25th.

Then, only twenty-four hours later, Dahmer made one of the biggest mistakes of his life.

Whatever poison was eating away at Dahmer's mind was not restricted to just murdering innocent men or defiling their bodies; it also involved a sexual attraction to minors—a troublesome fact for Dahmer, due to how society views child molesters and sex offenders.

However, it did not stop Dahmer from going ahead with his plans anyway.

Just one day after moving to his new home, Dahmer approached thirteen-year-old Somsack Sinthasomphone, in an attempt to take nude photographs of him. Even though the child agreed to go back home with Dahmer, later, he went to the police to report the murderer for having drugged and fondled him while he had been sedated. The killer had crushed sleeping pills and put them in Irish Cream, but they had only started to take full effect when the boy had arrived home. His father realized what had happened after interrogating his son.

Consequently, in January 1989, Dahmer was convicted of second-degree sexual assault and enticing a child for immoral purposes. The court suspended sentencing until May.

In March, while Dahmer awaited sentencing, he moved back to his grandmother's home. Ironically, despite the ax hanging over his head and the family's shock over what he had done, Dahmer still found time to kill again.

Dahmer's fifth victim was twenty-four-year-old biracial model Anthony Sears, who Dahmer met at a gay bar on March 25, 1989. Later Dahmer would state he had been at the bar merely to pass the time, with no intention of murdering anybody.

Unfortunately for Sears, he approached Dahmer with an innocent curiosity—exactly what Dahmer could not resist and used to his advantage. As Dahmer remembers, it was shortly before the bar closed, when Sears simply began talking to him. Dahmer found him exceptionally attractive. After a chat, Dahmer invited the man home—in spite of his grandmother forbidding him to do so. The two men performed oral sex on one another in the basement. Then Dahmer drugged and strangled Sears, repeating the tried and tested murder method he had used on his previous victims.

To dispose of his victim's body, Dahmer placed the corpse in his grandmother's bathtub and decapitated it, before unsuccessfully attempting to flay it. Eventually, he resorted to his typical method: stripping the flesh with a mix of potent chemical substances and pulverizing the bones soon after. He kept Sears' genitalia, as well as the man's head, and preserved them in acetone. They would be two of his most prized possessions for a long time.

The big day arrived on May 23, 1989. Dahmer's lawyer Gerald Boyle and Assistant District Attorney Gale Shelton faced off with attempts to defend and lock away the criminal, respectively. Both were unaware he was a serial killer. Shelton argued Dahmer did not appear to understand the full extent of his crimes, only seeing his actions as wrong because his victim was too young, rather than recognizing it was far more about the gravity of the act of drugging and sexual abuse. According to Shelton, this fact made Dahmer a dangerous individual. The D.A. wanted Dahmer put away in prison for at least five years, a sentence that would allow him to reflect properly on his crimes. Studies from psychologists supported this theory, demonstrating Dahmer was a manipulative and evasive character, who required intensive treatment.

Meanwhile, Boyle argued treatment was indeed needed, but without prison time. He cited on the positive side, Dahmer had kept his job and there was some normalcy in his life. He also emphasized Dahmer was not a multiple offender. Again, it is an example of the unawareness Jeffrey had killed five human beings by now—they had caught him before he had gone too far. To Boyle, "It was a blessing in disguise that Dahmer had been caught."

Dahmer was given a chance to defend himself; he was quick to lay the blame for his crimes on alcoholism. His manner of speaking convinced those in the courtroom. Dahmer made sure to act shocked, disappointed for what he had done, and repentant. He reiterated to the courtroom he had been able to keep a stable job and asked the judge and jury not to take this away from him. He said he wanted, "A chance to get help to turn his life around."

Safe to say, everyone was convinced. The judge stayed Dahmer's sentence and put him on probation instead of sending him straight to prison. He was also ordered to spend one year in the Milwaukee County House of Correction, under a "work release" regime. This allowed him to work during the day and return to jail at night. However, he was required to register as a sex offender. Jeffrey Dahmer was no longer as invisible as he wished to be.

During this time, Lionel was heavily involved in helping him out with legal costs and support. He still had faith in his son's recovery and yet another chance to start over. In Lionel's mind, Jeffrey was a "child who had slipped beyond his grasp, a little boy that was spinning in the void, swirling in the maelstrom, lost, lost, lost." He even openly opposed Jeffrey's premature release from the House of Correction, arguing that his son needed to be fully treated before he could harm others—and himself—even more.

The justice system ignored Lionel, the man who understood Jeffrey better than anyone else. Many innocent men would pay the price with their lives.

It had yet to be determined whether Jeffrey was a man who had suffered as a child and grown corrupt or was a terrible monster that took pleasure in defiling his fellow human beings. Nonetheless, confirmation was coming quickly.

Dahmer soon moved to another residence of his own. He would continue his murders into the year 1990.

The Milwaukee Cannibal was about to earn his name…

…in the worst possible way.

VII

Lost In The Maelstrom

AS PREVIOUSLY MENTIONED, DAHMER DID NOT fully complete his treatment upon his release; the judge granted him early release for good behavior. Dahmer, only ten months later, was a free man. Lionel even tried to stop this premature release by sending a letter requesting his son receive his complete treatment—for Jeffrey's own good—but the justice system ignored his pleas.

Dahmer found his way back into his grandmother's home by March of 1990, but once again, she asked him to find a place of his own to live.

That is how Jeffrey Dahmer ended up at his infamous address; Apartment 213, 924 North 25th Street. At Apartment 213, was where the most terrible part of Dahmer's story would occur; where Dahmer's monstrous nature would be revealed to the nation and world, once he was captured.

Dahmer took home his sixth victim just one week after moving in. The frequency of his murders was about to explode; he would end up killing men as often as once a week.

The latest man to become one of Dahmer's trophies was thirty-two-year-old Raymond Smith. He was a sex worker, who Dahmer lured to his apartment with the promise of fifty dollars for sex—a recurring trap in this tale.

Raymond accepted a drink from Dahmer without a second thought; if only he had known there were seven sleeping pills dissolved in the beverage. As soon as the effects of sedation kicked in, Dahmer strangled the man with his bare hands and took advantage of his corpse.

The next day, Dahmer went out and purchased a Polaroid camera. Returning home, he found a new use for his victim's corpse: posing Smith's body suggestively using it as a stimulus for masturbation.

After he finished taking the Polaroids, Dahmer dismembered the body in his bathroom. He boiled the arms, legs, and pelvis with Soilex—an industrial detergent—and then rinsed the bones in a sink. Jeffrey then separated the skull from the body, dissolving the rest of the skeleton in a container filled with acid. Keeping the skull as a trophy, Dahmer spray-painted it and stored it with Anthony Sears' skull, which he had brought with him from his previous address.

Just one week later, on May 27, Dahmer found his next victim. He lured a young man to his home, after having met him at a gay bar. Once there, however, Dahmer made a mistake; he accidentally consumed the drink he had laced with sedatives for his victim and ended up falling into a deep sleep. By the time he awoke the next day, the nameless young man had stolen several items and cash from him, but Dahmer never reported the incident to the police.

The next month, Dahmer lured a friend of his, twenty-seven-year-old Edward Smith, to his apartment. He drugged Smith and strangled the life out of him before wondering about the best way to preserve his corpse. Dahmer had already used bleaching techniques, but that weakened the bones and skull and made them brittle.

He decided to put the skeleton in his freezer for several months, hoping it would avoid moisture. Eventually, Dahmer realized the freezer did not stop the moisture-retention of the bones, and consequently was forced to dissolve the skeleton in acid. He placed the skull in his oven to dry, but it exploded suddenly and violently, becoming a useless mound of dust.

Dahmer later admitted he had felt terrible about killing someone 'pointlessly,' since he was unable to retain the man's body parts. In Dahmer's view, Edward Smith practically "did not count" for his personal record. No one was ever able to locate any of Smith's remains.

Three months after the murder of Edward Smith, Dahmer picked up twenty-two-year-old Ernest Miller. He met Miller on the corner of a street, luring him home with his typical offer of fifty dollars for his companionship. Dahmer asked Miller to let him listen to his heart and stomach, and he agreed. When Jeffrey prompted Miller for oral sex, Miller told Dahmer it would cost him a bit more.

Dahmer offered him a drink before they continued, and found he only had two sleeping pills remaining in his cupboard. Two pills would not be enough to sedate an adult male properly, so Dahmer would have to improvise. After watching Miller take the drink and then begin showing signs of sedation, Dahmer pulled out a knife and slashed his carotid artery open. The victim, visibly shocked, bled out within minutes. Dahmer went and picked up his Polaroid camera, taking pictures of Miller's dead body in several poses, before placing it in his bathtub.

Next, he severed the corpse's head. Later, Dahmer admitted to kissing and talking to the head during the dismemberment process. Dahmer removed the victim's heart, biceps, and other fleshy parts from the skeleton and stored them in his fridge in plastic bags. The terrible truth is that Dahmer wanted to consume the body parts later. He boiled the remaining flesh and organs with Soilex and rinsed the skeleton with the intention of preserving and keeping it as a trophy.

He bleached the victim's bones—the trick he had learned from an unknowing Lionel in his childhood—then painted and coated it with enamel, before placing it into the fridge.

Around this time, neighbors of 924 North 25th Street began complaining of foul odors coming from Jeffrey Dahmer's apartment. The building's landlord confronted Dahmer, and he apologized, stating he had a broken fridge and would get it fixed as soon as possible.

The lie served him well, and Dahmer did not have further trouble with the people in his building after that. Even so, some neighbors remained curious about the sounds of heavy falling objects, as well as the random hours at which a power saw could be heard coming from Dahmer's apartment.

Between September and October 1990, Dahmer met a twenty-two-year-old father, David Thomas, at a mall. He offered money in exchange for a few drinks, and a bit more if he agreed to pose for photographs. David was not aware of the photographs that Dahmer planned to take were of his corpse, so he agreed. Once at home, Dahmer provided Thomas with his special concoction, from which Thomas fell asleep soon after.

Once Thomas was out cold, Dahmer looked at him more closely and realized he had no attraction toward the man. He had suddenly lost interest in raping him. Dahmer began to think of what to do, but ultimately decided that letting Thomas re-awaken was too much of a risk; he strangled the man and dismembered his corpse. While dismembering him, Dahmer recorded the entire process with photographs and retained them, although he discarded all of the body parts.

Police would later show the pictures to Thomas's sister, who was forced to go through the ordeal of attempting to identify her brother.

Five months passed before Dahmer killed again. A dark cloud passed through his mind and his life. Suddenly, he began to fail at what he did best—charming men to lure them back home to kill. Depressive thoughts entered his mind regularly, and he considered suicide several times.

There is something to understand about Dahmer before we continue: he was not a psychotic case like many other killers. He was completely aware that killing was wrong and only truly enjoyed what came later—the defiling and dismemberment of their bodies.

Later, a neighbor stated that he had often seen Dahmer slipping into his own apartment guiltily—like a late-night thief—looking as if he was doing something wrong. Add the alcoholism and the fact Dahmer had shown strong signs of Asperger's syndrome since childhood, and it may be possible to understand him slightly better. His relationships never went further than a sexual encounter, and he was usually inept at getting to know strangers and forming bonds.

Dahmer was a rarity among young men his age, serial killers, and human beings in general.

Dahmer's social difficulties and obsession with paraphilias were never identified as part of a developmental disorder or mental health issue. Neither was it diagnosed or treated properly at any stage of his life. Dahmer, a confessed pedophile and secret serial killer, was as free as any other man, and he could do whatever he wished. That is, until someone detected and caught him.

That part of the story would take a while. In the meantime, unfortunately, Dahmer would take nine more lives. Despite the horrible acts our killer had already performed, the worst was yet to come.

Jeffrey Dahmer's horrific spree was about to reach its very pinnacle. The phase that everyone would remember him for was approaching.

Jeffrey Dahmer was about to die…

…and the alter-ego known as **The Milwaukee Cannibal** was about to take his place.

VIII

The Milwaukee Cannibal

IT WASN'T UNTIL FEBRUARY 1991—FEBRUARY 18, TO be exact—that Dahmer took his next life.

Cruising around the streets of Milwaukee, Dahmer came across seventeen-year-old Chris Straughter standing at a bus stop near Marquette University. He was an attractive model, which made it easy for Dahmer to entice him, using his most effective method: offering the chance to earn money by posing for nude photographs.

Curtis accepted. Halfway into their session of oral sex, Dahmer strangled the young man with a leather strap and began to dismember him. He had his Polaroid handy to record the whole procedure. Dahmer kept the victim's skull, hands, and genitals, as well as the photographs taken of each step of the dismemberment.

The next murder, however, would add an extremely gruesome detail to Dahmer's modus operandi. It will chill you to the bones.

As you may remember, Dahmer hated consensual intercourse because his partners moved and made noises, which he found distracting. Some psychologists believe Dahmer had always been in denial about his sexual orientation. They suggest this made him prefer silent, dead bodies that could not remind him he was having sex with a man.

For this very reason, Dahmer dreamed of creating "zombies." In his mind, these were creatures that had formerly been living men, but who Dahmer himself had transformed into mindless sex slaves, only living to serve his latest needs.

The focal point of Dahmer's first experiment involving this fantasy was Errol Lindsey, a mere nineteen-year-old.

Lindsey was heterosexual, but Dahmer manipulated him into visiting his house in exchange for cash. He became the first victim to go through the 'zombifying' process.

The chain of events started when Lindsey arrived at Dahmer's home. He was quickly drugged by the killer and did not open his eyes again until the ordeal was over. When he awoke from his long, sedated sleep, Lindsey felt weird. He informed Dahmer he was suffering from a headache and wanted to know the time.

Dahmer had used a drill to bore a hole into the man's skull. Then he injected hydrochloric acid into Lindsey's brain, in an attempt to permanently damage it. Dahmer felt insecure due to the victim's sudden awakening. He quickly sedated him again, then strangled and killed the youth before he could become a problem.

Dahmer decapitated the young man and kept his skull. He flayed the body and retained the skin in a saline solution. He would eventually have to dispose of it, reluctantly, when it became brittle.

On May 24, 1991, Dahmer met a man at a gay bar known as the "219 Club," which he had regularly used to find victims. His latest victim was an African-American named Tony Hughes, who was deaf and mute. At the bar, he communicated with Dahmer using writing and lip-reading. Dahmer lured the man home for sex and strangled him mercilessly, then carelessly leaving him to rot on his bedroom floor for the next three days.

However, just two days later, on May 26, 1991, a strange twist of fate took hold of Dahmer's life, bringing him the absolute closest to prison he had ever been thus far. First, it started when he met fourteen-year-old Konerack Sinthasomphone, who, due to coincidence or fate, was the younger brother of the boy whom Dahmer had been arrested for molesting in 1988.

He lured the boy to his home with an offer of money in exchange for taking some pictures of him in his underwear. Dahmer sedated Konerack using his trusty concoction and performed oral sex on the boy.

But more was to come.

As mentioned earlier in this chapter, Dahmer had always wondered about the possibility of creating "zombie slaves"—lovers who he could permanently take advantage of after putting them in a comatose state. He believed he could find a way to keep a man in a state between life and death, in which they could function at the most basic levels, responding to his every desire. His attempt to "brain damage" Tony Hughes had failed. Now he had another victim and was excited to experiment with this notion further.

Sinthasomphone would suffer the consequences of this curiosity that is obsessing Dahmer's mind. While the boy was sedated, the killer fetched a power drill, which he used to open a hole in the boy's skull near his frontal lobe. Not content with this terrible act, he began to pour hydrochloric acid into the hole in the youth's head, believing it would turn him into a mindless slave. The mix of acid and drugs made Konerack so detached from reality that even when Dahmer took him to his bedroom, right past Tony Hughes' body still laying there on the floor, the boy did not react.

Dahmer drank some beers as he lay beside the youth, studying the effects of what he had done to him. Eventually, he ran out of drinks and was forced to leave the apartment for a few hours. At some point, Konerack woke up...

...and escaped.

Konerack made his way through the apartment, cautiously at first, but soon found his way out of the building and wandered, dazed and nude, onto the streets of Milwaukee. Three women came across him shortly after. They approached to find the boy speaking in Laotian—a side-effect of the drugs, since Konerack spoke fluent English—and with no real idea of what was going on.

Unfortunately for Konerack, Dahmer was on his way back to his apartment when he spotted the scene and butted in, telling the women that Sinthasomphone was his lover and he had too much to drink and had gotten lost. The women did not allow Dahmer to take the young boy away. Instead, they called 911.

Two officers arrived quickly. Dahmer was suddenly in a very dangerous situation. Cornered, with two policemen about to go to his home, Jeffrey Dahmer had suddenly lost the upper hand.

IX

The Noose Tightens

THE TWO POLICE OFFICERS, JOHN BALCERZAK, who later would become the President of the Milwaukee Police Association, and Joseph Gabrish, arrived at the scene and intervened in what they immediately, and wrongly, concluded was an argument between two lovers.

Dahmer reinforced this opinion by convincingly stating the boy was actually nineteen-years-old, and often drank himself into such a state. Further, he added he had proof that would show young Sinthasomphone had willingly modeled for nude pictures. The three women were not as easily convinced. They told the officers to take a look at Konerack's buttocks, which were bleeding. The two law enforcement officers quickly shut down the women's requests. Instead, they escorted Dahmer back to his apartment, along with the now-covered, but still confused Konerack.

The walk back home was a nervy one, but Dahmer still acted as though things were under control. Once back at his apartment, he produced the Polaroids he had taken of Konerack, using them as proof the young man was with him consensually. The officers smelled something odd coming from Dahmer's bedroom, so one of them went to check it out. Dahmer must have felt great terror when the man entered the room where Tony Hughes's rotting body lay. However, the officer did not bother to do anything more than peeking his head around the corner.

The two men, now content with their search and not even having done a quick background check on Dahmer—which would have immediately revealed he was a convicted child molester—told the killer to take care of his lover and left his apartment. They even joked about it on their radio report. Dahmer finally breathed again, injecting his victim once more with hydrochloric acid to properly subdue him. This second injection was too much, and as a result, Konerack Sinthasomphone died.

Dahmer, content with having escaped an almost certain arrest, skipped work and spent the next day dismembering the two bodies. He preserved both victims' skulls in the freezer as trophies. He documented the dismemberment process and discarded the body parts.

A month later, on June 30, Dahmer met a twenty-year-old model, Matt Turner, at a bus station. He made use of his signature tactic that had served him so well: offering the model the opportunity for a professional photoshoot. It worked, and before long, Turner became Dahmer's fourteenth victim. In early July, Dahmer purchased a fifty-seven-gallon drum, which he filled with acid and used to dissolve Turner's body.

Five days later, Dahmer met twenty-three-year-old Jeremiah Weinberger, a Chicago resident. Jeff offered the man a chance to spend the weekend with him in Milwaukee, and after consulting with his roommate, Jeremiah accepted. They traveled together on a bus, arriving at Dahmer's home to have consensual sex and spend time together. Dahmer actually took a liking to Jeremiah, later stating the man was "exceptionally affectionate" and that "he'd been nice to be with." He didn't think of murdering him until Weinberger told Dahmer he wanted to go home.

As we have already learned, this was a trigger for Dahmer, who offered Weinberger a drink. The young man drank it, and once he was passed out, Dahmer drilled a hole in his skull. He injected boiling water in an attempt to turn him into a mindless slave, as he had with Sinthasomphone.

His plan half-worked: Weinberger fell into a coma and died two days later. Dahmer would remember this death—Jeremiah was his only victim to die with his eyes open. He placed Weinberger's torso in the fifty-seven-gallon drum to dissolve in acid.

On July 15, Oliver Lacy crossed Dahmer's path. He was an African-American bodybuilding enthusiast, who Dahmer enticed to his apartment in exchange for money and, again, the offer of a photoshoot. After they had sex, Dahmer quickly drugged and strangled the twenty-four-year-old, then having sex with his corpse. Dahmer decapitated and kept his head, heart, and skeleton. The latter formed part of a shrine he had begun to construct.

Four days later, on July 19, Dahmer was informed of his dismissal from his job. He had been absent from his position for too long. The killer did not take this well since his job had been the only constant in his life for the past few years.

Emotion took hold of Dahmer, and he went in search of another victim. Joseph Bradehoft, who was twenty-five years old and the father of three children, became his next victim. Dahmer strangled him and left him to rot on his bed for two days.

As it turned out, Joseph would be Jeffrey Dahmer's last victim.

Unfortunately for Dahmer, he had suddenly become sloppy, sloppy for a serial killer. Everything was about to come crashing down on him.

X

End Of The Road

" I THINK IN SOME WAY I WANTED IT TO END, even if it meant my own destruction." ~ Jeffrey Dahmer

Jeffrey Dahmer finished decapitating and cleaning Bradehoft's body on July 21. By then, the man's head was covered in maggots, but he preserved it and placed it in his fridge. Then, he put the victim's torso in a drum full of acid. Dahmer decided to move on to his next victim quickly. Now that he was jobless, his life had changed. He had more time on his hands than before and less control over his urges. Things were going to get ugly, fast.

The very next day, Dahmer went in search of his next victim. He approached three men, offering them one hundred dollars to join him at his apartment. He told them he would take nude photographs of them, and then they'd drink beer and simply spend some time together. Only thirty-two-year-old Tracy Edwards agreed to join him, and the two went back to Dahmer's home. Once again, Dahmer's chosen victim was African-American, a fact that would later be given significance by those who tried to understand Dahmer's sick mindset.

As he entered Dahmer's apartment, the foul smells and sights immediately assaulted Edwards' senses. There were boxes of hydrochloric acid lying around. He suddenly felt very uncomfortable. When Edwards turned to look at Dahmer's fish, which the killer pointed out in an attempt to distract him, Dahmer moved quickly and handcuffed his wrist. He then unsuccessfully attempted to cuff Edward's wrists together. He took the thirty-two-year-old to his bedroom to take nude photographs. Edwards caught sight of the fifty-seven-gallon drum and identified it as a possible source of the ugly odor. He was no fool. It was obvious the strange man who had brought him to this apartment was disturbed in some way.

Edwards had no time to think of an escape plan; Dahmer pulled out a large kitchen knife and threatened to stab him if he didn't cooperate with the photography session. Edwards was quick to unbutton his shirt, attempting to calm Dahmer down—telling him he would do whatever Dahmer said. This seemed to work. Dahmer began to get distracted watching television as Edwards finished opening his shirt. In doing so, he was already looking for a way to get out of there and alert somebody—anybody—who could save him from this terrible situation.

Once Edwards was naked, Dahmer approached him and began to listen to his heart intently. He ran his knife along the victim's skin and told him he was going to consume the precious organ. Judging by what he had seen in the room, Edwards knew the stranger was not bluffing and that his life was going to be over very soon. He tried continuously to convince Dahmer that he was a friend, but the killer had already made his decision.

Edwards asked to use the bathroom, and Dahmer accepted, but the killer was waiting patiently when the victim stepped back out. Edwards knew he had to find the perfect moment.

And finally, five hours later, it came.

It was almost midnight. Edwards asked to use the bathroom a second time. This time, he noted a lapse in Dahmer's concentration. The killer, for all his caution, had not secured Edwards' handcuffs. Edwards knew it was time—he smashed his

71

fist into Dahmer's face and kicked him in the stomach, knocking him off balance, running out of the apartment building and onto the streets, before Dahmer could make him pay for it.

Two police officers looked up, greeted by the strange sight of a man with a handcuff on one hand, and shouting at them. Eventually, they calmed him down long enough to get his story; a "weird dude" had lured him home and placed cuffs on him before threatening to kill him with a knife.

The officers agreed to accompany him back to the "weird dude's" apartment. They reached Apartment 213 and knocked on the door. A pleasant, thirty-one-year-old blond man opened the door and allowed them inside. He listened as Edwards recounted his accusation. Then he admitted that he had indeed placed the handcuffs on the man's wrist and offered to retrieve the key to free him from the device.

One of the officers told him to back off and went to Dahmer's bedroom himself, where he spotted the large knife Edwards had described. He also noticed an open drawer with pictures. On closer inspection, the officer saw Polaroids of bodies in different stages of dismemberment, and body parts in various arrangements. In a horrific realization, he noticed the decoration and background in the photos were identical to the ones around him. The police officer left the room and showed the pictures to his partner. Now Dahmer's calm demeanor disappeared; the demon was unmasked.

In an attack of desperation, Dahmer threw himself on to one of the officers attempting to resist arrest and avoid being cuffed. The two men managed to subdue him and place handcuffs around his wrists. One of them pinned him down while the other began searching the apartment for further evidence of what he had done. It did not take long—upon opening the fridge, Officer Rolf Mueller let out a loud scream, slammed the door shut, and yelled, 'There's a fucking head in the refrigerator!'

Dahmer looked up from the floor and knew it was over. The officer had seen the skull, and organs packed in plastic bags and glass jars.

With Dahmer's time finally coming, the guilt inside rose to the surface.

"For what I did, I should be dead," he said softly, just loud enough for the police officers to hear him over the sound of the second squad car approaching the building.

After the police had taken Dahmer away, a detailed search began within Apartment 213 of 924 North 25th Street. Police would find three more severed heads in the kitchen. Seven skulls, some spray-painted or covered in enamel, some bleached, were found in his bedroom. They found two human hearts swimming in blood at the bottom of Dahmer's fridge, along with an arm muscle on one of the shelves. Within his freezer, they discovered an entire torso, a bag of organs, and some flesh. While this was shocking enough, there were two entire skeletons hidden in a different part of his apartment and a pair of severed hands. Dahmer had stored two preserved penises alongside a scalp, and inside his fifty-seven-gallon drum were three partially-dissolved torsos.

To worsen the horror even further, police officers collected seventy-four Polaroid pictures from Dahmer's drawers, documenting the endless stages of more than a dozen dismemberments. Others showed his victims' corpses in provocative positions that were somewhat erotic. It was the worst kind of photography the police had ever encountered. Although these images would haunt their every dream, it was only through these very Polaroids that police were able to identify the victims.

Once at the police station, a detective named Patrick Kennedy questioned Dahmer. He would spend the subsequent weeks getting answers and details out of him. The killer believed that it was time to put an end to the horror he had created. He waived his right to an attorney. He admitted to having murdered sixteen young men in Wisconsin, and one in Ohio, in 1978. He confessed he had killed Steven Hicks due to his teenage fantasies. He disclosed that the man had tried to leave after sex and that had pushed his buttons the wrong way.

The confession led to an exhaustive investigation by the German Police, who wanted to make sure Dahmer had not killed anybody while serving the Army within their nation. Eventually, they corroborated that he had not.

When asked about the procedure he had used, Dahmer described how he strangled most of his victims after drugging them, while in some cases, he had injected their skulls with acid or boiling water. He told the police he frequently had sex with the corpses or masturbated on them, although this was optional.

Further, he described putting each body in erotic positions, typically with the chest thrusting outwards. The dismemberment, he explained, would follow soon after, and was often accompanied by a step-by-step documentation using Polaroids. Dahmer said he found cutting open his victim's torso and revealing the organs sexually arousing, especially when feeling the heat the dead body produced. He remembered every single procedure except for Steven Tuomi's. Dahmer said he was not sure how Tuomi had died; if he had been unconscious or not before the fatal beating. He did recall placing the torso over his bathtub to drain the blood, before removing the organs he did not want to keep.

Dahmer recounted how in disposing of the bodies, he experimented with various chemicals and acids—an attempt to find the best way to reduce the flesh and bone into a foul-smelling sludge. Then he could pour it down a drain or toilet. Dahmer confirmed retaining other parts he wished to consume or keep as trophies, and also admitted to having consumed the hearts, livers, biceps, and parts of thighs of several victims.

In his sick mind, Dahmer believed the victims could 'come alive again' within him. He even tenderized and seasoned the meat before eating them to give them an extra taste. Dahmer said that it gave him an erection to consume human flesh, although human blood was not to his liking.

Even after all of this horror, a shocking revelation was still to come. When asked why he kept so many bones, Dahmer revealed that he had been in the process of constructing an altar dedicated to many of his victims. He wanted to decorate it with the entire skeletons of some victims and the skulls of others. Dahmer believed the altar would allow him to "draw power" from his victims' bones. He admitted that, if there was an evil power in the world, then perhaps he had been heavily influenced by it, to commit these acts.

On the 25th of July 1991, Jeffrey Dahmer was charged with four counts of murder. The following month he was charged with another eleven murders. On September 17, he was charged with the murder of Steven Hicks, after the remains he had discarded in his childhood home's woodland backyard were found. He was not charged with the attempted murder of Tracy Edwards. He was not charged with the murder of Steven Tuomi, because he had no memory of this crime and no physical evidence was found.

On January 13, 1992, he pleaded guilty by reason of insanity to fifteen counts of murder.

By using an insanity defense, Dahmer was seeking an easy way to earn pity from the judge and jury.

It was not going to work that easily. Dahmer had committed too many evil acts. Things were not going to end well for him.

Justice was coming for Jeffrey Dahmer, just like it should have decades before. His tale was going to end as it began…

XI

Final Twist

TENSIONS WERE AT AN EXTREME HIGH. GIVEN that the majority of Dahmer's victims had been African American, there was a strong belief by the public that his murders had been racially-motivated, so security measures had to be taken around his trial.

The justice system installed an eight-foot barrier of bulletproof glass in the courtroom to protect Dahmer, and heavy security escorted him at all times. The fact that only one African American person sat on the jury also increased the tension.

As for the killer himself, Dahmer's insanity plea turned an already complicated case into a shit storm; to put things bluntly.

It added a new focus to the case of a man with 15 murder charges and was at the center of media attention. The media now asked: was Jeffrey Dahmer insane? How else could he have committed such horrific and inhuman acts against innocent victims?

The defense immediately began its battle to prove that Dahmer was, at the very least, suffering from a paraphilia; necrophilia, and his strong dependence on alcohol, and borderline personality disorder were powerful enough to drive his impulses and obsessions to an uncontrollable point.

Dahmer was also finally diagnosed with a psychotic disorder, a condition that would help the defense explain why he had committed acts so detached from human nature, such as cannibalism.

The prosecution was certain that Dahmer was not insane at all. He had all the signs of a calculating killer, who knew exactly what he wanted and worked towards his goal; submissive partners who served to satisfy his dark sexual desires and required nothing else from him. He was not a sadist either, instead simply using his victim's death as a vehicle for getting to his paraphilias of necrophilia and cannibalism.

The prosecution also argued that Dahmer had worked hard to find ways to lure his victims into solitude, where he could kill them easily and without detection, a fact that spoke of preparation and planning.

Dahmer's alcohol abuse was also pointed out repeatedly, with one forensic psychiatrist noting how the killer required a level of intoxication before he could kill. This fact, the prosecution argued, suggested that Dahmer was very uncomfortable with murder, and found the need to drown his inhibitions before being able to take a life.

Another expert said that Dahmer was killing gay victims because he hated them, just like he hated the homosexuality within himself. This expert also agreed that Dahmer was not insane, but instead extremely cunning, handsome, and able to manipulate a victim with ease.

On February 14, both counsels finished giving their final arguments, and the jury met to make a decision. While the decision was not unanimous, the majority dismissed the theory that Dahmer was not in control of his actions when he had committed his crimes.

The jury concluded the best place for Dahmer to end up was not a hospital, but a prison cell.

81

The court prepared to hear the verdict the very next day.

Dahmer was ruled to be sane and, above all, guilty of his crimes. He was sentenced to life imprisonment plus ten years for his first two counts of murder, while the remaining thirteen counts brought him a sentence of life imprisonment plus seventy years. If anything, he was lucky they would not execute him; the State of Wisconsin had abolished the death penalty one hundred and thirty-nine years prior.

As if the fifteen counts of murder were not enough, Dahmer was also tried not long after for the murder of Steven Hicks, this time in Ohio. The hearing was brief. Dahmer exited the court with a sixteenth and final term of life imprisonment on May 1, 1992.

Just to put this into perspective: Dahmer had been sentenced to a total of **nine hundred and fifty-seven years** in prison.

Dahmer said goodbye to his parents—who had been there at every stage of his trial—and was taken to the Columbia Correctional Institute in Portage, Wisconsin. There, for his own safety, he would remain in solitary confinement.

This procedure was implemented despite the fact that he made it clear on several occasions that he wished to be dead. He even told his mother he did not care if anyone attacked him. On one particular occasion, just two years later, a fellow prisoner attempted to slash Dahmer's throat with a makeshift weapon made out of a sharpened toothbrush, but it did not accomplish more than some superficial wounds on Dahmer's neck.

Dahmer slowly earned the trust of the guards and other prisoners and began spending more time with them. Prison authorities even assigned him janitorial work. He became comfortable. Part of him wanted to start over, so he found his way to the path of God and became a born-again Christian.

Even so, nobody wanted to see a man who had done what he had done becoming comfortable. In fact, there was one particular prisoner who wanted him dead more than any other. This prisoner was an African American, who had read about Dahmer's black killing spree. He believed that God had asked him to cleanse the evil from the world. And Dahmer was evil—no doubt about it.

The prisoner's name was Christopher Scarver.

Scarver had seen Dahmer in the mess hall and watched him playing with his food, pretending the pieces of chicken were body parts and the ketchup was blood. He had also found a newspaper reporting on Dahmer's crimes. He cut out the article so he could confront the killer and ask him why he had committed such horrible crimes.

He finally got that chance in 1994.

On the morning of November 28, 1994, Dahmer was assigned to work with Jesse Anderson and Christopher Scarver to clean the prison gym showers. They were all unshackled.

At one point, one of the two men poked Scarver in the back with a long object of some sort. This angered him, and he turned to see both men laughing at him under their breath. Dahmer then proceeded to clean elsewhere, giving Scarver the chance to follow him.

In Scarver's mind, his actions were justified because the guards knew he hated Dahmer and had still put them together, alone, in the same place at the same time. With no guards around to watch, Scarver felt this was tacit vindication for his plan, a sign. He was still carrying the newspaper article in his pocket.

Before confronting his prey, Scarver picked up a dumbbell from the weight room, ironically, the very same weapon Dahmer had chosen to kill his first victim, Hicks, in 1978.

Dahmer heard the man approaching from behind and turned around. He saw Scarver, with a piece of paper in one hand and a dumbbell in the other. Somehow, Dahmer knew what was coming.

Scarver described what followed in a recent interview:

"I asked him if he did those things 'cause I was fiercely disgusted. He was shocked. Yes, he was... He started looking for the door pretty quick. I blocked him."

With two swings of the weight, Scarver crushed Dahmer's skull.

"He ended up dead. I put his head down, Scarver said."

Not content with having rid the world of Jeffrey Dahmer, Christopher Scarver then went for Anderson and caved his skull in. Unlike Dahmer, Anderson suffered for two days before dying.

It was all over.

Jeffrey Dahmer—murderer of seventeen men, necrophiliac, child molester, and the man known as the Milwaukee Cannibal—was dead.

It would not bring any comfort to the families of the victims, nor would it make him any less famous to the public, but Dahmer was now gone from this world, unable to repent for what he had done or at least pay for his crimes.

The young boy who had been lost in the maelstrom at such a young age was now truly gone...

...forever.

Conclusion

"I SHOULD HAVE GONE TO COLLEGE AND GONE into real estate and got myself an aquarium, that's what I should have done." ~ Jeffrey Dahmer

The aftermath was huge. Dahmer had sent massive shockwaves through the lives of hundreds with his actions, and now they had to pick up the leftover pieces of their shattered world.

Dahmer's mother, Joyce Dahmer, asked the media if they were happy now that her son was dead. She also wanted to know if they were glad that he had been bludgeoned to death. She died of cancer in the year 2000, having attempted suicide on several occasions. Dahmer's brother, David, has since changed his name and lives in anonymity.

Lionel Dahmer grieved for his son for many years, even writing a book about his and his son's story. Proceeds from the book were sent to victims' families as compensation. He and his wife Shari live in Ohio.

Dahmer's assets were awarded to the families of his victims. His possessions were destroyed and buried in a landfill at an undisclosed location.

The Milwaukee community took part in a candlelight vigil on August 5, 1991, to share their feelings of pain and anger over Dahmer's murderous deeds. Over four hundred people attended in an excellent show of support for one another

The Oxford Apartments were demolished in November 1992. The land ended up as a vacant lot, after plans to convert it into a memorial garden failed.

In 2007, evidence surfaced that linked Dahmer to the murder of Adam Walsh in 1981. A police investigation followed. It was eventually declared Adam's father was correct in believing that another serial killer, named Ottis Toole, had been responsible. Toole had died in prison in 1996.

Tracy Edwards never recovered from his ordeal despite becoming a hero for his part in Dahmer's capture. He became homeless in 2002, after many encounters with the law involving drugs. In 2012, he was sentenced to eighteen months in prison after being involved in the murder of another homeless man.

As for Jeffrey Dahmer, his terrible tale lives on in the media, books, films, and television documentaries, which have continually studied both his mindset and motives. He was a unique killer with a strange sense of guilt hanging over him. Even as his crimes became increasingly heinous, he was aware that he was doing something evil but unable to stop.

In a way, many believe that he is not that different from the rest of us, in terms of his upbringing.

However, one can also argue that Dahmer's guilt over his actions and his awareness of reality may make him even more depraved than other killers. While many psychopaths experience a separation from reality and a lack of complete awareness of the damage they are doing to their victims, Dahmer was fully cognizant of the impact of his depraved behavior.

The case of Jeffrey Dahmer is proof that not all serial killers are the result of abuse and trauma. His story suggests that children must be properly supervised and helped along the road to becoming good, law-abiding adults.

Acknowledgments

This is a special thanks to the following readers who have taken time out of their busy schedule to be part of the True Crime Seven Team. Thank you all so much for all the feedback and support!

Joan, Lisa Millett, Jamie Bothen, Pamela Culp, Barbara Davis, Patricia Oliver, James Herington, Linda M Wheeler, Bonnie Kernene, Derrick Langley, Jo Donna Hoevet, Tonja Marshall, Kathy Morgan

Continue Your Exploration Into

The Murderous Minds

Excerpt From Ted Bundy

I

The Birth of a Psychopath

EVERY MONSTER BORN INTO THE WORLD IS AN
innocent, screaming baby—Ted Bundy was no exception. On
November 24th, 1946, our killer was born Theodore Robert to
Louise Cowell in the city of Burlington, Vermont. In regards to his
father, nothing certain can be said—it has never been determined,
despite Louise claiming on the boy's birth certificate the father had
been a salesman and Air Force veteran. There were rumors among
the family that Louise's own dad may have fathered the child, but
no evidence was ever produced supporting this claim.

Whichever the case, Louise moved into her parent's house with
the newborn Ted, and lived in Samuel and Eleanor Powell's home

for three years. During this time, they began feeding Ted a lie—one he wouldn't know the truth of for many years—primarily due to social stigma and old-fashioned beliefs. The trio of adults agreed to make everyone believe Ted had been born to Samuel and Eleanor, and that his mother Louise was his older sister. These lies would go on until Ted reached his college years; the rage of being lied to for so long may have contributed to developing his psychopathic disorders.

Within the Powell household, Samuel was an abusive tyrant. In spite of initial claims that Ted had been close and looked up to the man, his family would later admit the grandparent had been extremely violent, bigoted, and regularly spoke to himself. Bullying at home was so powerful that Eleanor aged into a depressive, withdrawn, old woman who required periodical electroconvulsive therapy to treat her mental state.

Young Theodore watched this all through confused, infant eyes and it definitely affected him. At one point, he surrounded his aunt Julia with kitchen knives while she was sleeping. Then he stood by her with a grin until she awoke. While this is a disturbing behavior for any child, the fact that Ted was only three years old when it occurred, made it that more disturbing.

When Ted was four, Louise decided to move to Tacoma, Washington, where her cousins, Alan and Jane Scott, lived. This would be where Ted's young life would develop and his first run-ins with the law would occur; although they were minor offenses and showed no sign of a soon-to-be serial rapist and killer.

A year after the move to Washington, Louise met a hospital cook at church and they instantly fell for each other. The man, Johnny Culpepper Bundy, formally adopted Ted as his son, soon going on to have four children with Louise. Ted was always distant, feeling uncomfortable around Johnny and the children, and would state later that he had never liked him.

Ted's own recollections of his teenage life were memories of reading crime novels and magazines for stories and scenes that included sexual violence and maimed bodies, as well as peeping in women's bedroom windows. Ted's mother would claim he was an excellent son who never forgot a special occasion to gift her with something; he often spoke of his dream to be a policeman or a lawyer. Classmates also remembered Ted as a friendly, well-known student, yet Bundy claimed to biographers he had never grasped the concept of friendship.

Ted Bundy's behavior soon showed sociopathic signs and a general disregard for the law. Breaking into cars, Ted would steal objects he found inside with the intent of selling them. He was also quite skilled at shoplifting, taking advantage of it to support his skiing hobby. Ted was arrested, at least twice as a minor; however, the details of the incidents were expunged from his record as soon as he reached the age of eighteen.

Ted was done with high school by 1965 and began studying at the University of Puget Sound. He did not like it there because his classmates were all from wealthy backgrounds and it made him feel inferior. After a year, he transferred to the University of Washington, where he studied Chinese. At the same time, he looked for simple, minimum wage jobs; he never lasted longer than a few months at a time. Whether it was working as a grocery bagger, shelf-stocker, or volunteer at a Seattle suicide hotline, his superiors remembered him as an unreliable and untrustworthy young man. Ted also volunteered in political activities for the Republican Party, such as Nelson Rockefeller's presidential campaign of 1968.

It was around this time that Ted met the woman that would perhaps become the most pivotal of his life, even more so than any of his unfortunate victims. Although he had never been a model boy, things were about to turn a lot uglier in Ted's young life.

The End of **The Preview**

Visit us at **truecrimeseven.com** or **scan QR Code using your phone's camera app** to find more true crime books and other cool goodies.

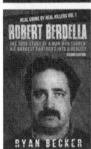

About True Crime Seven

True Crime Seven is about exploring the stories of the sinful minds in this world. From unknown murderers to well-known serial killers. It is our goal to create a place for true crime enthusiasts to satisfy their morbid curiosities while sparking new ones.

Our writers come from all walks of life but with one thing in common, and that is they are all true crime enthusiasts. You can learn more about them below:

Ryan Becker is a True Crime author who started his writing journey in late 2016. Like most of you, he loves to explore the process of how individuals turn their darkest fantasies into a reality. Ryan has always had a passion for storytelling. So, writing is the best output for him to combine his fascination with psychology and true crime. It is Ryan's goal for his readers to experience the full immersion with the dark reality of the world, just like how he used to in his younger days.

Nancy Alyssa Veysey is a writer and author of true crime books, including the bestselling, Mary Flora Bell: The Horrific True Story Behind an Innocent Girl Serial Killer. Her medical degree and work in the field of forensic psychology, along with postgraduate studies in criminal justice, criminology, and pre-law, allow her to bring a unique perspective to her writing.

Kurtis-Giles Veysey is a young writer who began his writing career in the fantasy genre. In late 2018, he parlayed his love and knowledge of history into writing nonfiction accounts of true crime stories that occurred in centuries past. Told from a historical perspective, Kurtis-Giles brings these victims and their killers back to life with vivid descriptions of these heinous crimes.

Kelly Gaines is a writer from Philadelphia. Her passion for storytelling began in childhood and carried into her college career. She received a B.A. in English from Saint Joseph's University in 2016, with a concentration in Writing Studies. Now part of the real world, Kelly enjoys comic books, history documentaries, and a good scary story. In her true-crime work, Kelly focuses on the motivations of the killers and backgrounds of the victims to draw a complete picture of each individual. She deeply enjoys writing for True Crime Seven and looks forward to bringing more spine-tingling tales to readers.

James Parker, the pen-name of a young writer from New Jersey, who started his writing journey with play-writing. He has always been fascinated with the psychology of murderers and how the media might play a role in their creation. James loves to constantly test out new styles and ideas in his writing so one day he can find something cool and unique to himself.

Brenda Brown is a writer and an illustrator-cartoonist. Her art can be found in books distributed both nationally and internationally. She has also written many books related to her graduate degree in psychology and her minor in history. Like many true crime enthusiasts, she loves exploring the minds of those who see the world as a playground for expressing the darker side of themselves—the side that people usually locked up and hid from scrutiny.

Genoveva Ortiz is a Los Angeles-based writer who began her career writing scary stories while still in college. After receiving a B.A. in English in 2018, she shifted her focus to nonfiction and the real-life horrors of crime and unsolved mysteries. Together with True Crime Seven, she is excited to further explore the world of true crime through a social justice perspective.

You can learn more about us and our writers at:

https://truecrimeseven.com/about/

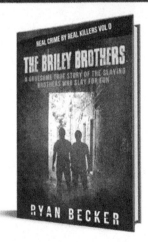

Dark Fantasies Turned Reality

Prepare yourself, we're not going to **hold back on details or
cut out any of the gruesome truths...**

Made in the USA
Monee, IL
06 August 2024

63423024R00059